The Flowers Will Bloom

Cynthia Rodriguez

Instagram- @poetry.by.cynthia

copyright © 2025 Cynthia Rodriguez.
All rights reserved.
No part of this book may be used or reproduced in any manner whatsoever without written permission except in the case of reprints in the context of reviews.

Also by Cynthia Rodriguez
Within The Walls
Becoming Spring Again

To those who searched for ways to hurt me and deemed me incapable by choosing to follow the mental health stigma—
I thank you.

Because of you, I finally had the courage to write this book.

And for those who are struggling or have struggled—
to my fellow mental health and anxiety sufferers:

this book is for you.

Dear reader,

You are about to engage in quite a journey with me—one that will be quite dark.

I chose to keep many of the poems in this book dark as I feel it keeps them honest. The truth is, when we're in those moments of pain we feel hopeless. We don't want to be, but those moments are our reality.

Some poems may seem depressing and speak of suicide.
I advise you to please read with care.
My intention in touching on this topic is to let others who are—or have been—in the same position know that they are not alone.
When you are depressed and broken, you feel as if no one understands you.
Keeping these moments in my poetry dark allows me to show others that they are not alone.
The darkness in those poems may not show a light at the end of the tunnel, but in my opinion, feeling seen means a lot.
There is hope in knowing you are not alone.
I don't want others to feel broken, but it is a reality—many do.
In some of my writing I chose to not sprinkle any hope,

as I felt it would take away from the reality of those moments.
For those who are or have been completely hopeless, I felt you would feel most seen in the darkness of my poetry.
Sprinkling that little bit of light might make some people feel misunderstood, as their lives are currently only dark.
Many of my poems stay dark and hopeless, because that was my reality in those moments.
And I know it is also the reality of others.

Among the dark poetry, there are poems sprinkled with hope—
and poems that serve hope as the main course.
So it's not all about pain.
There is light as you read on.
But as much as I'm rooting for you to make it out of the darkness,
I also want you to know I feel you.

You are not alone.

Let's grow together.

I hope you feel seen through the words of pain, and you feel spoken to through the words of encouragement.

Table of contents

No escape

Brave heart

Removing the thorns

Reflection

Letters to heaven

The flowers will bloom

No escape

I was just four when I watched my cousins' amused faces
as they took turns flicking at my belly button—
like a game of ping pong.

I should laugh too, right?
They're playing with me.

Wait, I'm not the player; I'm the game.
I wonder why my belly button is not the same.
Why does mine stick out while theirs sink in?
Why am I different?

This was just the beginning.

insecurities

You sit there and pick out everything you think is wrong with me.
I say nothing but silently agree.

I've always seen things I didn't like, but now they terrorize my mind.
And you bring your match and ignite.

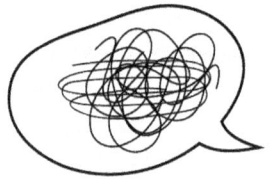

People tell me I'm too skinny.
They tell her she's too curvy.
Well, why can't both be pretty?

Why do you have to believe I'm struggling?
I'm doing just fine.
It's just my body type.

But they don't stop if you're not pleasing in their eyes.
And suddenly I'm not worthy in mine.

With all this agony stuck in me, I want to release.
I want to breathe.
Scream so they hear me.
But instead I bury it inside, and I don't speak.
And this anxiety has no mercy.
Calls upon all my insecurities to see.
So they can also take their shot at me.

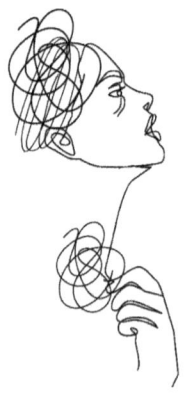

My tongue is indented.
My teeth pinned it down and left it printed.
And my heart was racing, banging on my chest, screaming,
Let me out!
And its roots weren't strong enough to hold it down.
I saw it jump out of my chest and run away.
You should have seen the look on everyone's face.
Has their heart never done the same?
Relax is all they would say.

If only it were that easy.

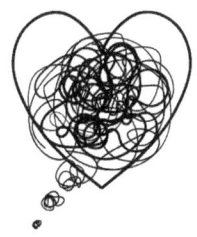

Murky clouds, midnight howls.
The moonlight's shine hides tonight.
The starless sky evokes somber thoughts to the mind.
It's like every mistake I've made is in a line,
and they take turns slapping me in the face.
I can't hide or run away.
If I do, they engage in a chase.
And it's one I can't escape.

The night seems never ending.
I close my eyes, sing to my mind lullabies.
I tell it to hush, but it just won't stop.
I can't silence the cries.
So much noise, but it's just me alone with the night.
Yet my mind and I can't see eye to eye.
And my heart watches in tremor as we fight.
I search for sunlight, but it seems to be taking its time.
It feels as if hours go by, but dawn never arrives.

I feel the memories stick like the midnight mist.
I wash it off, but the night continues to carry on.
And it turns into dense fog.
Everywhere I go I'm followed by my thoughts.

Every turn leads darker into the night.
But as I stare at the clock, I realize it's been hours since sunrise.
But I still can't see the light.

Without warning it strikes me in the chest.
I feel it force itself up my throat in its knotted form and back down into my stomach where it settles for a vacation.
Telling it to leave is not an option.

I dig my fingernails into my palms and sink my teeth into my thumb.
My perspired face is now flushed.
The room moves and fills with fog.

One moment I forget to breathe, a moment later I feel like I just ran a marathon and the following moment I forget how to breathe.

    anxiety

The thunderstorm will be arriving soon.
The rain will come pouring down.
You're thinking if you stay you'll drown.
But you're in way too deep to turn around.

Every single night I cry myself to sleep.
Praying that I have beautiful dreams.
But instead I'm met with nightmares about all the bad things that could happen to me.
My heart is drowning from the pain from my past, present and grief.
But it's the future I wish to see that gives me hope to believe.

Waking up to another day.
Hungover from the pain of yesterday.

Already getting drunk on the sorrows of tomorrow.

Wondering when the worry will fade.
How many sleepless nights will it take?

You ask,
who taught you to be a pessimist?

I respond,
my life experiences.

It's either you crash every time or fall from reaching so high.
But it's never just to enjoy the ride.
And that perception becomes a new aspect of my life.

I watch as dense fog strangles the stars, all while I feel your cruel words do the same to my heart.
And the moon shines its light despite.
But your spitefulness has a tight grip that dims my might.

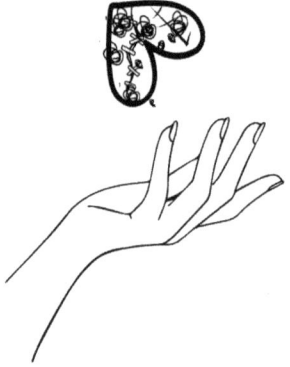

Your laughter echoes through my mind.
It kept me up last night.
Tranquility, I tried to find.
But there was nothing but you in sight.
I felt you crawling on me like dust mites.

I tried to brush you off.
Tossed and turned hoping you would stop.
But you lingered in the air.
Screamed louder in my ears.

How do you manage to stay and simultaneously be miles away?

I hear you impeding my sleep again.
I keep locking the doors, yet you still creep in.
And I thought it was the wind howling, but it was actually you screaming.
Your claws against the walls screeching.
I tell you to leave, but you refuse to concede.

I turn on the light, but I still see memories of my cries.
Where do I go? Where do I run to hide?
I've already shut you out, but you still invade my life.
Your cruel lies, such a sharp knife.
And you'd do it again, time after time.

Remember what it's like to laugh uncontrollably?
Stomping our feet on the bus floor—not worrying about what everyone else would think.

That was our happy.
We didn't care how we seemed.
What a joy it was when we were free spirited teens.
Life really became a reality.

It's getting hard to breathe.
And I know I've made it this far, but I've become so fragile and weak.

I don't know if I will make it out alive, or if my heart will resign.
And I don't know how much further I can go.
Broken on the inside, might even wish I wasn't alive.
This pain is too much to deny.

You give it your best fight.
But still no sign of light.

Do you remember when you called me ugly?
It was a Monday,

        Tuesday,

                Wednesday,

                        Thursday,

                              Friday,

                                    Saturday,

                                            Sunday.

You told me to kill myself.
I was already hanging from the cliff's edge, and you stomped on my fingers that were gripping for dear life.

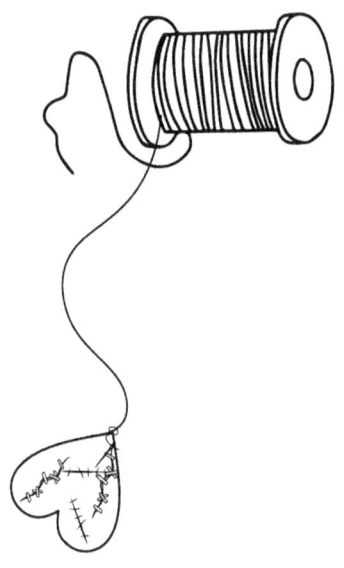

Sometimes words can be the bullets that load the gun.

Your serrated words cut me deep and left me bleeding.
Did you even care that you left me hurting?

I wonder if a dragon's mouth burns when it shoots fire.

Because then I'd ask,

with the flaming words you speak, does yours ever hurt?

And if a dragon could speak, why use fire when it could use words

Won't let them see you cry.
You just want to deny.
Don't want to let them know they're a part of the reason you hide this pain inside.

I wish I could forget about all this distress, as if it never existed.
Let it be something that drifted.
Let this hole in my heart heal, like it was never even real.
Just a nightmare that I had.
Something that never went bad.

Because it's just too hard to let go when these scars are always there to let you know.
And my mind eats my soul.
My heart wants to be no more.

Instead of letting go, I want to let go.

At nearly 500 days, the gates of my safe haven, I'm forced to leave.
A mandatory meeting.
It took everything in me.
The streets thought they were dreaming.
The sun stopped shining.
The clouds went gloomy.
They all couldn't believe what they were seeing.
But the venture was only momentary.
I went back, and 297 more days I stayed.

All my friends stayed, even when I pushed them away.

Eventually, I had to allow myself to wither so they couldn't find me.

The flowers in the garden scream my name.
They're excited to see me.
They know very well if I turn to dust, so will they.
The grass sticks its tongue out hoping for rain.

And the trees dig their roots deeper into the ground.
Even nature struggles to survive this drought.

I try to push the haunting thoughts out of my mind.
But they keep gripping tight.

Some people get butterflies in their stomach.
I get a swarm of bees.

When you're next to me there will never be a drought.
My tears will always provide.

Don't get too close, or you might drown.

You don't believe you're good enough.
You desire to live, but instead you let life pass you by.
You tell yourself one day it will be alright.
But in the meantime you have to hide.
Never let anyone see you cry.
Do so well wearing that disguise.
But that doesn't stop everyone, they still criticize.
They narrate your entire life and pretend to know why.

I wear a mask everyday.
A smile that fades as soon as you look away.

I was just one step away.
But the current drew me farther in.
Maybe it was a step I was never meant to take.
Maybe a joyful life just isn't my fate.

Now I'm sinking.
And I'm so tired of fighting.
My strength is now dying.

And I no longer want to fight it.

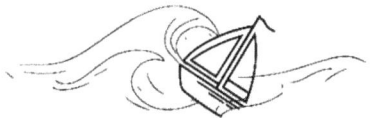

When I'm so close, I feel so far away.
I'm like a ghost walking the halls of yesterday.

Because I don't know how to just let go.
All these memories haunting me, they've got a strong hold on me.
I just want to go to a place where I can be free.

Let go of all the worries that are keeping me down.
Because every time I get back up, I'm reminded of
what it's like to be on the ground.
No matter where I run, there doesn't seem to be a way out.
No one can hear me when I shout.

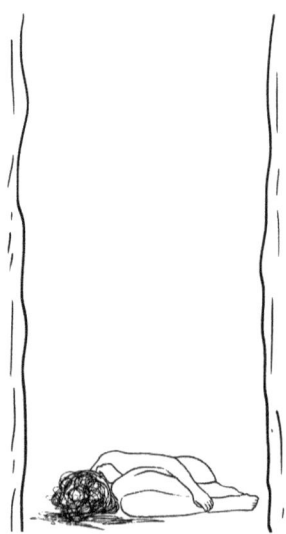

Every time I drift a little into hope, the current once again drags me back in.

I'm in disguise right now.
Because I'm trying to hide the pain inside that you caused to ignite.
But happy is difficult to portray when I'm in flames every day.
Not so easy to put up a facade.
But incognito I go forcing the fake, like it doesn't hurt, your betrayal's crushing weight.
So I choose to smile today as it is still easier than finding an escape.

I wish I could undo it.
But instead I'm left drowning in my regrets.
And I'm forced to consume these memories every day.
I just want to find a way to numb the pain.

I am no longer broken—
I am shattered.

I don't know how I've made it this far.
Since so long ago I should have fallen apart.
Thought life would be easy, but it's only been hard.
Guess that was little naive me.
My heart has taken the worst of this beating.

The sun will rise, but sooner or later it will set.
All that happiness will be consumed by darkness.

I try to fight it.
But it's scarred inside me.
I try to push those thoughts out.
But they keep pinning me down.
I want to escape my way out.
But the longing future is with doubts.
At arm's length from it yet unreachable somehow.

I'm left broken.
All because of words spoken.

Bottled up inside.
Looking for a reason why.
But instead I'm left with another sleepless night.
Never-ending cries tormenting my mind.
Sanctuary I wish to find.
But each and every time the pain ignites.

Waiting for the right time.
When will it be the time?
I'm tired of saying I'm fine.
And everyone pretends they don't know it's a lie.

I just want to let go of it all.
No more echoes through these walls.
No more pretending I never fall.

I'm trying so hard to run away.
But I can't find a destination.
I'm struggling to find a path.
And I'm being haunted by the past.

I feel like an ocean without waves.

A bird without wings.

A floating soul with nowhere to go.

A smile can mean a lot of things.
A smile can be a disguise.
A way to hide pain.
A smile can be a lie.

Monday

Tuesday

Wednesday

Thursday

Friday

Saturday

Sunday

Broken glass.
Pieces at my feet.
You still don't see me.
I'm the reflection on the concrete.

Laughter can be a distraction.
A way to escape this place even if it's just momentary.

But it can also be used to conceal your blues.

I try so hard, but this darkness has blinded me.
Even in the light I can no longer see.

Even in my healing, my heart keeps on remembering.
It screams with my mind in synchrony.
I wish I could just tell it to leave.

It feels like my heart, head and stomach are all engaged in a ruthless battle with one another.

Sitting on this bench waiting for it to end.
But I still can't make it past from where it begins.

I saw a light from far behind me.
But it was dimming.
Could have sworn it was running away from me.

The hope was being vacuumed from inside me.
What was I supposed to believe?
With every fall it becomes harder to get back on my feet.
Dense fog was becoming thicker, making it difficult for me to see.

I was begging on my knees.
But even if this rain would flee, my own tears could drown me.
On the ground I got used to contemplating.

I'm barely breathing.
I mean my heart is still beating, but I'm suffocating.

I want to cry no more.
I just want to shut my eyes and sleep peacefully.
No more worrying or nightmares about all the bad things that could happen to me.

Hoping for a change.
Trying to find the will to keep my strength.
Looking for a reason to stay.
I've had enough of the teasing.
I just want to drift away, fall asleep and let go of this pain.

It breaks me down.
I try to get out.
I pace around.
I scream and shout.

But no one can hear me.
Because I'm screaming internally.
In silence I ~~live.~~
In silence I exist.
I try to survive it.

But the water keeps rising.
I fear soon I'll be drowning.
Once I get exhausted of swimming.

Can I write this pain away?

My heart is breaking.
My soul is aching.
It's from these open wounds that I continue to bleed.
And the scars become memories.
Reminding me of the pain like a broken bone when it rains.

No one knows, I've kept it a secret for so long that it's gone cold.
I sit and watch the memories unfold as the pain grows and grows.

How do I break through, let all this pain go, forget about it, leave it behind and never rewind?

How do I do that, and never look back?

Complications arise.
Happy faces in disguise.
I guess we're all trying to get by.

Stolen chances
Failed promises.
I guess that's where my heart lies in regret.

Pain is my best kept secret.

Somebody asked me the other day,
what's the biggest lie you've ever told?

I replied,

that I'm okay.

Lights that burn your eyes, tears you've cried are now burned inside.

Words of encouragement fade.
It's the bad things that stay.
Why does it have to be that way?
Why can't I say,
I've got scars of happiness?

Another day has dragged me into the night, out of the sunlight.
I watch as the skies cry.
Watch as they tear the ground apart.
I feel their tear drops as they flood my heart.
Speak to the moonlight.
Hide from the sunshine.
Seek hope in the stars.

The features of the night tend to lie.
The stars give off a beautiful shine.
The darkness is brightened by the moonlight.
But a storm will be coming, it's just a matter of time.

Please don't ask me how I'm doing.
Because I'll just lie and say I'm fine.
And you'll be too ignorant to see what I hide.
But guaranteed you'll see it's a misery of a life.

Can't understand how I could live this way?
Well jokes on you, because I've never lived a single day.
Survival is the only way to get by.
I'm in pain all the time, but it's not that easy to escape.

I can jump, but what if it's into the abyss.

I've got pieces of me shattered everywhere.
You can go on and try to help collect them, but you might just get cut.

You speak such cruel words to me.
You tell me no one enjoys my company.
And I already have about a million insecurities.
So your hostility is the whipped cream.

It's on days like this, where my struggles hang high.
And hope is far from reach.
I reflect on all the opportunities I let pass by.
At this point in life, this isn't where I thought I'd be.
A blissful life I thought I'd see.
But now, not even in my dreams.

You left and I stayed.
Not a word in mind to say.
Not even a goodbye.
Just walked away.
But left me with haunting memories to last a lifetime.

Do you ever feel like you won't manage to get by?
Life is hard, and it can get dark.
And you don't know which way to turn.
It's all a blur.
Just when you think you've seen the worst, you fall once more.
Even deeper than before.

Now it's a longer way back up.
You wonder if one day your strength won't be enough.

Heart breaks, soul aches.
Where do I go from here?
Wish I could disappear.

I threw the painful memories out, but they echoed on their way down.

And it must have been the abyss, because they never stopped.

I feel like a deflating balloon.
Gradually losing my helium.

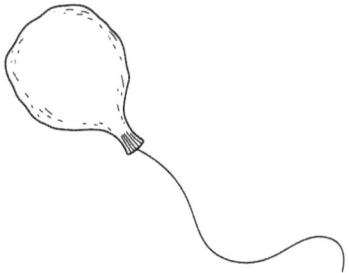

I finally escaped the big bad wolf.
But then 20 more came after me.

I feel so empty yet so full of pain.

It's like a hand is being held out to me.
But it's actually pushing me further down the hole.

Was it fun for you?
I don't know why you say and do the things you do.
Does it leave you amused?
You break my limbs one by one.
Rip my heart out with your bare hands.

Maybe you just wanted me to crawl so people could see you help me stand.

Such a nurturing person you are.

It's another one of those days.
No matter how hard I try, I can't release this pain.
My heart still suffocates.
I still can't find my way.

I try to hang on to hope, but these wounds won't close.
It's all so difficult.
Longing to let go.

You knew that the house I'd never leave.
You made some ***joke*** that the delivery man I'd marry.
Sent his picture around on your phone like some parody.

*But it's just **comedy**.*
No hostility.
It's just fragile little me.

And I never got an apology.
I was already hurting.
You didn't need to stab your knife so deep.
I get there's a lot you don't see.
But what you did should never have been mistaken for comedy.

I'm just waiting for these windows to break.
Because I can't take this pain.
It's the only thing of me that remains.
I don't know how this weather it's sustained.
Because it broke everything else in me.
But my windows somehow remain standing.

And I know it's all I have to shield me.
But it feels as if it's too late.
I'm tired of losing the race.
I've dealt with everything I've had to face.

But now it's time for me to run the opposite way.
Or stop resisting, and let it pull me away.

I wake up in the morning, looks like mom's got visitors.
I guess until they leave, my room I won't be leaving.
Even if that's until evening.
Sometimes it's even until the sun sets.

And I hear them talking about how I must be crazy.
Asking why I'm always hiding.

What a mistake I made telling you how I felt.
You only made it about yourself.

This is why it's easier for me to just smile.

Why do people light a candle for me if it's just to blow it out?

Did you even care to know I was hurting?
You threw gasoline on me when I was already burning.

And you break me just to mend me and be able to say,
I made you.

What a day I've had.
Traveling everywhere in my head.

The sun said goodnight.
The moon returned to light the sky.
But I can't seem to make it back.

I want to leave all this noise for the night, wash myself clean from all the filth you spit on me, sip some tea and fall into sweet dreams.
I don't even remember what it's like to sleep.
Because lately it's been you haunting me.
When my insomnia finally sets me free, it's still you that I see.
And I want you to leave, but you've got your tight grip on me.

You make it clear you'll be staying the night.
I want to run, but I feel paralyzed.
And even if I could move, there's nowhere to hide.
You fit in every crack no matter how tight.
They say to just tell you goodbye.
Shut off the lights.

What they don't know is that you thrive in the dark.
And even then you're there when I shut my eyes.
You fuel up on my fright.
I wish it'd be that easy to tell you to let go of me.
Tell me now, how much is the ransom for my tranquility?

Where is the button?
I cannot find it.
How can it be that something this loud doesn't have a way to bring the volume down.
There must be a button to shut my brain off.
A way to make it stop.
I don't want to think of all the cruel things you have done to me.
But my brain keeps on remembering.

Everyone here is laughing.
They all find you amusing.

Each one even takes a turn at being the comedian.
And I am the subject that is being viewed as merely an object.

This pain I can't escape.
Because your words are trapped in my memories from when you threw them at me without thinking about how they would leave me hurting.

Because you say no harm was intended.
And that you can't control the way I intake.
But you're still guilty of voluntary ignorance.

Because how could you believe that telling me all those things wouldn't hurt?

When you see that I'm at my very worst, will you still continue to say it was my intake?
Because I will not take the blame.
Yes, we should try to not let things get to us, but we're human at the end of the day.
Tell me now, if someone punches your bruises with full impact repeatedly, will you resist the pain?
I really don't think so, even if you try to be brave.

I don't expect him to stand up for me.
I don't expect him to give up his pride.
Because in his mind his reputation will ignite.
Even though I'm the one in flames.
And to everyone he'll let it be some game.

You could throw gasoline on me, and he would hand you the match.

I try to be brave, but sometimes it's just too hard.
I try to keep it all inside, but then I collide.
I don't let them see me cry.
Do my best to hide.

But words are always being thrown at me.
People say hurtful things.
Humor is what they call it.
They don't acknowledge.

I ache inside, but they're the ones with a heart that's sadder than mine.
Because it can be cold at times.

Sometimes I feel hope can be deceiving.
If it's not meant to be, it will never be.

Each marking represents a mistake.
But none justify how much I gave.

Does it make you laugh when you lie?
Does it bring you joy as the pain intensifies?

You left these scars in my heart.
Now I'm feeling so alone and so cold.
You dropped me so low in this dark hole.

Does anyone even know I'm here?
Because even though voices sound near, the light is so far away.
It looks like there's no escape.
Seems like even if I try I won't make it out on time.

My heart aches in ways I never thought possible.
I feel your claws embedded deep trying to excise it from me.
You leak a vile fluid onto me that is not washable.
As my heart clings to me, I feel your claws sinking.
It burns from the acid you keep on spitting.
I beg you to release it, but it's clear you want it to stop beating.

My frail body struggles to stand in the pit you threw me in.
My bruised knees trembling.

My heart is a mess right now.
I pray to God for an out.
But every turn leads to a darker route.

Venomous words keep striking.
Shame to those who choose no antidote.
You choose to let your mind be poisoned to your liking.
Don't even care if your greed burns me.

Forget all the good deeds.
There's a new outbreak called money.
The symptoms will make you kill just to get a piece.
And you'll be more than willing.

It's been 28 days since we last spoke.
You expressed how much you loved me.
I expressed the same for you.
You said I was a good person.
I never thought the one to take a turn holding the knife would be you.

I always thought you knowing my heart wasn't just hope.
I thought you'd know those rumors are lies you're being told.
But as we said goodbye to a precious life, we also buried a bond that tied you and I.
I guess that's the end of our bloodline.
Everyone else has a tie except for us five.

Now we are just the forsaken.
Perceived as remnants that will always be insufficient.

Losing you was one of the greatest losses I had from this.
I understand where your loyalty is.
But never the injustice.

You ask,
how's life?

And I wish I didn't have to lie when I look you in the eyes and tell you, *good*
        followed by
                I'm fine.

I see the ocean waves getting higher everyday.
And I pray to God that he gives me strength to keep on swimming.
Keep the will alive in me.
Send the current away.

If a star fell from the sky for every lie you told, well then there'd be no stars left for the universe to hold.
And the stars would lose their home, just like your heart lost its soul.
It used to be a heart of gold, but now it's crimson from all the blood shed of all your victims.

You showcased your hands as a nest, inviting my heart to rest, but they were bottomless.
And I fell into your ruse.
Deception at its best.
You disguised your abrasiveness with a soft caress.

But your splinters began to peek, and they pricked my heart lifeless.
But you didn't stop, not even at my death.
You used my tortured heart as a shop, set it up for your cultists amusement.
Made me the attraction at your sick museum.

Where my blood continued to drip even after my heart became stiff.

My heart sinks deep from all the weight of entanglement of you.
I want to be free, but you dig your claws into me.

Every lie that you say is a laceration to my veins.
Leaving me to bleed out for days.

You give up your morals for my pain.
And you'll stab me all over again.

I'm starting to believe if I don't bleed, you don't feast.

They take my blood, but it turns out they also want my soul.
Nothing will fuel their thirst, they'll always want more.
They sink their teeth into me like they've done this before.

And they hold me hostage every night with their cruel stares.
And I know I shouldn't care, rumors are a craze everywhere.
But how will my wounds heal when all they do is take my heart and tear and tear.
And they cut deep with their sharp glares.

Never even gave me the opportunity to speak.
They don't care about integrity.
They just have to feed the hungry beast called greed.
And the real fortune is my blood, because that's the greatest thing they're inheriting.

Look at you throwing those rocks at me.
I'm already down, fragile and bleeding.
Yet this one seems to be larger than the last one.
Won't you have mercy?

Are you waiting to hear me scream, from the taped up cracks from my broken walls?
Because you won't let me stand tall.

You diminish my all to nothing.
Tell me, does that make you happy?

You don't even care about the truth as long as it benefits you.
If it rewards, you'll execute.
Greed dictates your next move.

You won't even hear what I have to say.
Forget the witch trials, you want me dead either way.

Stormy winds and heavy rainfall in my mind.
Wish I could teleport back in time.
Nothing seems to make it right.
Greedy people never get satisfied.

Treasures in the sky.
Buried behind murky clouds.
The map is written in the sky, but it's hard to find.
It's like a dream right in front of you yet far from reach.

The feeling you have lost before the storm is even over.

defeat

The memories haunt me.
Every wound resurfacing.

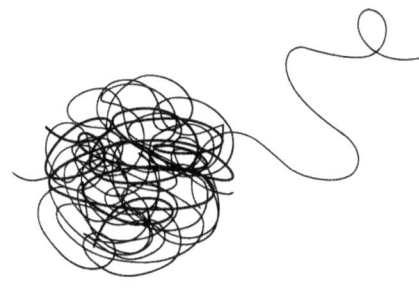

Echoes of you call my name.
I hide away, but you keep searching.
Crying for mercy is useless as you have become so hard-hearted.
You run around, knife in hand.
And your followers shadow you submissive to your command.
No matter how spiteful, they remain loyal to your demands.

And I wonder if they believe your lies or if they just love the taste of my blood.

2 AM, could have sworn I saw you at the edge of my bed.
I reach for the lights, but you're nowhere in sight.

I try to comprehend what's going on.
Why are you here even though you're gone?

I demand you leave, but you lay right beside me.
I know it will be another night I won't sleep.
And if I die it will be brutally.
Because you deprive me of my sanity.

And you said my tranquility was yours to keep.
Declared my thoughts your prisoner and said I would never be free.
And you'll do anything to watch me become nothing.

We laughed, we cried, we did it all.
But now I wonder if it was all worth the fall.

You led me up the highest mountain and didn't stop until we reached its peak.
And everything was the way I had dreamt it'd be.
Wasn't prepared for what you would do to me.

You held my hand as we stood at the very top, looked away and pushed me off.

You left me in the cage, but not before I set you free.

I feel the pain everyday.
Because you don't take a break.
You stab me repeatedly.
And you sharpen your blade in between.
Tell me now, is my helpless body on the floor bleeding what you desire to see?

You find your way in.
Burn me even though I'm innocent.

They slayed me.
Accused me of blood sucking.

But I was innocent.
They even kept the dagger in my neck in case I'd rise from the dead; I'd be decapitated.

They cut me where I'm already cut.
Stabbed their sharpest knife into my open wounds.

The same wounds that were once scars, then wounds over scars, scars over wounds, wounds over scars. They cut, and I bled, and cut, and I bled, and cut and I bled.

You leaned to comfort me, but your touch was abrasive.

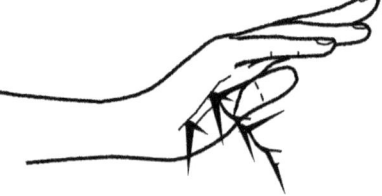

To live in a fantasy world.
Where pain doesn't exist.
Wouldn't that be a bliss?

A place where the grass would twirl.
Flowers blooming with beauty that was out of this world.
Even petunias would be perennial.
A place where happiness is perpetual.
Fields of lavender growing for miles.
You'd swear you saw the honey bees smile.

Children reading their favorite books under trees.
The river clear and glistening.
Sunflowers dancing and spinning.
Butterflies in all your surroundings.
A place so magical that all your previous troubles would vanish.
Even bunnies would sing praise in happiness.
The unimaginable happiness.
A fantasy world where pain is unknown.

Where is that place?

Heaven

Can I go now?

I demanded my heart it be silent.
But it wouldn't hush.
It continued to pump blood, faster and faster.
And each pump grew wider and wider, beating at my chest, beating at my lungs, leaving me gasping for air.
And my mind pleaded with it to be silent as the noise of my insides screaming in agony it could not bear.

But my heart refused to concede.
And the weight began to fall heavy.

I had no choice, I had to do it.
I gripped my hands around it tightly.
And I demanded it not breathe.

But I didn't succeed.
My heart ever so stubbornly continued to breathe.

I felt your warm skin turn cold.
And saw your warm tone turn pale.
Never even got the chance to get your color back from the poison in those treatments.

I saw your full cheeks sink in.
Your body destroy its own organs.
Wish the only side effect was that you would have made it.

I heard your once strong voice turn frail.
Witnessing so much pain and adversity has me wondering if we're already living in hell.

And only the chosen get to leave.

I watch as you go.
I feel myself drowning in the pouring rain.
The lightning strikes me repeatedly.
But I'm still standing.
And it pains me.
I don't want to be.
Because what's worse than dying, is dying every single day and then reviving.

And what was in that little pink bag of yours couldn't take your pain.
But as I'm drowning, I see it as my escape.
And it was about 200 ways.
I feel my body come to ease as I'm swallowing.
And I felt it happening just as I was swallowing.
I don't even know where I went, because it was so peaceful I saw nothing.

It was a sudden release of all my agony.

An impulsive and regretful thing.

Where was my soul supposed to go, when I saw yours slip away?
How was mine supposed to carry on and stay?

Out of my body I watched it float.
Unable to bear how I watched you go.
I see my soul traveling through everybody.
But I have no control.
No way to navigate.
And it's like everyone is speaking in a foreign language, but my mind translates.
So I can hear their words, but I can't relate.
I don't belong.

I saw my soul leave me.
But my stubborn heart, it won't stop beating.
Despite everything I did to my body.
It still loves me.
Even though I tried to murder it with oxy.
I tried to strangle it when it wouldn't stop crying.

You said give it 6 months.
As if grief has an expiration date.
Surely there are other ways of expressing empathy.
Rather than to give grief a shelf life.

I also ask, how is it that grief gets better with time?
Does it not make sense the more time you are without a loved one, the more you miss them?

If someone you love goes on vacation for a year without communication, do you stop missing them after six months?

Why is it that if someone is alive we're allowed to miss them for as long as they are gone, but we have to miss someone who has died less and less?

They say time takes pain, but that isn't true, because everyday I still miss you.
I still have this hole in my soul.
And it's bound to grow.
Because even after rainbows, life still brings thunderstorms.
But I've learned to cope.

I've learned that it may be a sunny day today, but tomorrow it may rain.
That's just life.
And its ways.

You pray to the skies to send you a sign.
You say goodbye to yesterday.
But will tomorrow be okay?

I wish I was a star in the night sky.
Shining ever so bright.
No one would know that was a life.
Just a speck of white.
No worries to cross my mind.
Just a beautiful thing that lights the sky.
No tears to cry.

And I wish I was a candle.
I'd be the light that guides, through the night.

Brave heart

So far things haven't been so great.
Let life slip away.
Said maybe it was just my fate.
Maybe I was never meant to make it past the gates.
And that even if I held on it'd be too late.
I held on to, *it will be okay.*
But I still haven't found my way.

But I think I'll stay.
Set my hopes up for one day.

I wish I didn't have to wait for all this pain to pass and have it all go away in a snap.
I wish I could make the darkness go away and have the sun shine all day.
How I wish, but I can't.
Because I can't make today tomorrow and yesterday today.

Battles are meant to be fought.

I was broken yet unbroken.
Because you left me bleeding, but somehow I'm still standing.

It's like the strength in me is slowly draining from all these open sores.
I say I can't take it anymore.
But I should know by now that I have been here before.

And I survived.

The lights were dimming, and my hope was fading.
I could feel every painful memory being embedded deeper into me.
And my heart wanted to leave my soul.
But my soul refused to let go.

How is it that every time my heart dies it revives?

My brave heart just won't stop beating, even though I continue bleeding.
It won't give up on me.

How is it that I still get up every time I fall, and feel like I've got nothing left at all?
I look for healing, but it seems so far from me.
Yet somehow I still go for the reach.

How is it that I'm still standing after the thunderstorms have left me torn?
How is it that the heart I believe is so frail, is actually strong, a warrior?

Memories are the scars left in me from where I was once bleeding.

I bled away until my body was left cold.
But my heart wouldn't let go.

Even after repeatedly saying I have given up, I find myself fighting.

Why is it that I stand tall even when my knees are weak,
yet my courage is overseen by me?

I wiped the tears from my eyes today.
Cleaned the surface but on the inside I am stained.
These scars inflict continuous pain.
And I try to push through, but I can't bear the emotional weight.
Please make it stop, don't take me and please take me,
I've prayed.
Will it ever go away?

I say my doubts out loud.
I'm ready to let it consume me.
I even want it to.
But then,

I get back up again.

I'm taking it one day at a time.
And it's my soul that screams from the unhealed wounds in me.
My mind that keeps me up at night.
But it's this brave heart of mine that won't give up on life.

Removing the thorns

I waited for you on the bench that day.
I thought you were just running late.
But it turned out it wasn't that way.
You couldn't be a man and handle things face to face.

And I waited.

I waited with the rain.
I waited when the darkness came.
I waited when the anticipation drove me insane.
I waited when I began to fall into a deeper ache.
I waited even when I became numb to the pain.
I waited after being awakened and having it happen all over again.
I waited after hearing the chilling sounds of my heart break.
I waited even though I knew for me you'd never do the same.

And now your hands rest, blood stained.
The weapon—a dagger.
The blade— your words.
They'll haunt me til it's the death of me.
But not a sound will be heard.

I'm in way too deep for anyone to hear me.
Even my echoes are too faint and will be perceived as the cries of the wind.

And you keep my heart against the wall pinned.
Your trophy, your big win.

But you were only able to reach my heart because I gave it to you.
I threw it out in the cold, just to keep you warm.
When your words became fire, I let it burn.
My poor heart pleaded with me to set it free.
But I didn't listen, as I didn't love me.

You made me believe, when you chose to stay with me.
You held me so close.
And promised you'd be there even through the worst.
You pointed at the brightest star and said it was ours.
You said when I'd get lost it would be a light always guiding me.
Now I can't look at the sky without remembering.

Why do you stay even when you leave?
I hear a song, it's your favorite melody.
I turn around, a family portraying a future I had once seen.

I'd ask you to go, but you're already gone.
But you're like a ghost.
Continue to cling on.
Haunt me the most.

But I don't want you here anymore.
I've held on for so long.
Confused and distraught.
Stuck in where did it all go wrong.
But I'm the one with the key to the lock.

It doesn't have to stay this way.
I just have to be brave.
Slay a few demons on the way.
Open the doors to a better place.
And you can't stay.

I come to find that you're willing to confine me in your box of prejudices.
You don't care if I drown as long as you make it out.
You know the truth, but you choose the worst of you.

Tell me now, am I the first person whose head you've shoved under water?
Or are there more?

How many victims keep you up at night with their screams?
And if it's just me, well then I want you to know that the praise you received for your dishonesty is yours to keep.
But the heavens always see.
They see your loyalty lies with greed.

And I never expected you to stand by me, but you didn't have to shove me under so deep.
Would you be willing to stand with dishonesty if its intention is to stop when I no longer breathe?

How are you feeling, they ask.
Depleted, I reply in my mind.
But instead I smile and say, I*'m fine.*
And my sunken eyes can't lie.
But most people just hear and don't look.
They let you read your own book.
And I read to them the opposite of what I hide.
Truth is—

My stomach is a knot.
It's constantly rolling past my esophagus into my throat where it stays stuck as I gasp for air.
I try to swallow to force it back down, but it seems I have forgotten how.

I remind myself to eat.
No wonder my stomach wants to leave.
And my mind is jailed with all those cruel words you speak.
But let me start comprehending that the problem is also me.
When my mind wants to stray I shouldn't let it seek.
It's easier to say than do, but at least I'll know I'm trying.

I won't let them dictate when they can stay.
And I won't let them leave me vacant.

We live in a world so cold.
I try to be bold.
But my heart's not made of stone.
And my heart can break just like a resilient linen can be torn.

And you just go around saying the things you say, assuming I'm unbreakable anyway.
Or is it your ignorance saying you can't control the way I intake.

Yes, I have some control of letting things get to me, but at the end of the day, I can still bleed.

An ignorant person lacking empathy—

someone who is not blind to knowledge; they simply refuse to see it.

Sometimes people say things they don't think about.
They just let the words flow out of their mouth.
And others are just thinking out loud.

But the ignorance is still the same.
You have to watch what you say, because your words can be the source of someone's pain.

Pain that words can inflict are always overlooked by the ignorant.

Ignorance is in the air.
It's caught up in everyone's hair.
It rapidly spreads and is highly contagious.

Will your antibodies view it as foreign?

Ignorance takes place.
Did you forget that I'm human?
I'm not a robot, and I'm not made of steel.
I see just as much as I feel.

Try to avoid those things.
But eventually it will get to me.

Because anybody who says that they can get hit over and over again and feel nothing, well I don't believe them.

Thick skin may be layered over my heart, but that won't erase my scars.

If you don't want to accept what you did, well then that's fine with me.
But don't give me some artificial apology.
So insincere, telling me you're sorry, but you can't control my feelings.

As if it were my fault for feeling pain from your hurtful words.

The moment someone says, *but* after saying,
I'm sorry,
Know that they are not truly sorry.

Bullying someone over your own insecurities, well that's not a decent thing.
Do you just like to let it stream?
Or do you do it for comedy?
Well I don't find your jokes funny.

I see you getting high off ignorance.
I bet you want another hit.
Strike me again, but this time you'll miss.

If it makes you feel good, if it makes you feel big, well then go right ahead and laugh at the courage I have gained.
Come around like a hurricane.
But standing I will remain.

Those were my tears falling from the sky.
The lightning strikes, the howling winds were my cries, keeping you up at night.
Tell me now, are you feeling sleep deprived?
Were you trembling in fright?
Did you worry you would drown as my tears flooded right before your eyes?

And all the hail that came was from all the rocks you threw at me.
Did it make you wish you hadn't played so dirty?
You gave up your integrity and created a storm from all your cruelty.

He's a beast, but he's also a hustler.
Works hard to get his blood money from doing his dirty deeds.
Has his followers at his feet.
Only comes out at night so people can't see.
Walks in daylight protesting equal rights.

But it's just a disguise.
He serves the dark side.
And I'm starting to see his darkness shine.
It's too great for him to contain inside.
I can see the greed in his eyes.
His mouth spews bile from all his lies.
He wears a rosary around his neck, but it's from there that I hear his prisoners cry.
He believes he's a mastermind.
But his evil cannot hide.

He's the one that loads the gun but will never pull the trigger.
Instead he summons his henchmen and guides their finger.

Then they all have a feast.
They toast with our blood to getting what they need.
They know they won't survive if their greed doesn't eat.

I tell you the truth.
But you don't even care, you just want to believe what benefits you.

Let me ask, is your tongue prisoner of your vicious mind?
Does it plead with you to stop?
It must burn from so many lies.

Does it entangle itself in a knot but is forced anyway?
Because it's only an occupant of the space.
What your mind demands, your mouth says.
So your dark, dark thoughts are the ones that lead the way.
And you say that I need to pray, but I do pray everyday that this all goes away.

Because I know angels see the truth in the words I speak.
But what about you?

You said I need a little bit of heaven, but your mind is the one that's king of hell.

I thought you were being fooled by all the lies.
But I now see you're also the master mind.

He's king of the ring.
He's the one that you feel, but you don't see.
Pretends to be a friend, but he's an enemy.

You should be ashamed as angels see your game.

You're like a vulture; you let others do the dirty work.
But some are not satisfied with roadkill.
They want a fresh meal.
So they'll be the king and take the lead.

I see you running red lights,
thinking you're invincible and you'll defy.
But when it's green you're paralyzed.

On red you want to go.
On green you stay idle.
Where were you this whole time when you should have hit the gas on that green light?

Now you're reckless when you drive.
But you'll end up crashing with your own lies.

I once thought that you had the devil on your shoulder feeding you those vicious thoughts you act upon.
But I now see that you are actually possessed by the devil of greed.
Tell me now, how can I set you free?
Your evil is slowly killing me.
Did they take you as a prisoner, or did you volunteer willingly?

I feel my intestines being strangled by your lies and deceit.
How do you eat?
Do you sit at the table with your family and pretend you are eating my tortured heart as a treat?
Is that what gets your appetite going?

Do you imagine the pain I must have endured to have a heart so ruptured?
Do those thoughts make you crave more?
Do you lick your lips as you taste the anguish in my blood?
Is your favorite part the moment my heart tore?
Does it bring you delight as you hold your glass out to my bleeding heart and watch it flood?

How is it that your soul has become so depraved?
Did you fall or jump into that pit filled with snakes?

Will you allow for your evil to be exorcised, or are you living your best life?

I hear your footsteps at night.
I hear you feasting on my walls like termites.
I put up concrete, but you just went in every crack seeking.

Tell me now, do you hear me screaming, begging you for mercy?

Do my cries keep impeding, or do you sleep peacefully?

You set out a platter of delectable lies.
Their lips water at the sight.
The irresistible sweetness gives a powerful urge, that's a toxic lure.
But it is also one they do not try to fight.
Instead your lies are devoured.
And they crave more.

Do you own what you say, or do you say it without thinking?
Do you love who you are, or is it a mask in disguise?

Shiny rocks have blinded you.
You don't even care to seek the truth.

Sometimes I stop and think,
how could this be happening to me?
I was the only one to step up and get things done.
And because I did you didn't have to.
You may have even viewed it as me taking a burden off you.
And this is your gratitude!?

I hear you in this desert heat, echoing how you would be
my sanctuary.
Your broken promises still linger in disbelief.
You put a bandage over my grief.
But I should've known you knew I needed stitches.
Now you left me here to bleed.

I never thought it would come to this.
Your betrayal hurt more than those
triple scorpion stings.
And the venom in your words keeps finding its way in.
I feel you crawling on my skin.
My body fights to resist, but as I wipe you off your
residue sticks.

This blazing sun is blinding me.
I feel my body burning, yet I'm shivering.
I hear every drop of sweat amplified by your deceit.
My body is giving up, but it's my mind you still have to
defeat—*The one you portrayed as weak.*

I see the vultures waiting me out.
I bet you thought I'd be dead by now.
But I will not be a carrion.
You'll have to eat me alive.
You can go ahead and send the coyotes at night, but I will

still fight.

Hope is the last thing to die.
And it's been my dagger and my light in many other lives.
They've killed me before, but I always revive.

It used to be good between you and I.
Tell me now, have you forgotten those times?
Because I could have sworn you would have never put me in a bad light.
Trust me with your life, as I would have with mine.
Wish you had told those lies, *nice try*.

Blood is the bind, but greed is the knife.

Words of encouragement on my hospital bed,
I never thought you'd be the one to want me dead.

You've already drained me.
But that still hasn't quenched your thirst.
You show me your teeth.
It used to be a warm hand you were offering.

Now you've gone so cold.
What did they do to you?
You're so far from the truth.
Your newfound cupidity has blinded you.

There you go again, like a daredevil.
Desperately doing careless things.
Running with your web of lies.

Didn't your mother teach you not to run with scissors?

I must admit you really hurt me.
You didn't care to help stop the bleeding.
You came around so friendly.
Gave me an apple to eat.
I never thought you'd be this deceiving.

My blood is on your hands, but do you feel me in your dreams?

Do you sleep peacefully?

I'll take the long road.
It will take me half the amount of time more, but the shortcut is filled with liars and deceivers.
There's a serpent that begs you to feed her.

Then she takes her strike.
Her venom is one of a kind.
It's her trickery that packs the might.

I see it was so easy for you to throw me out.
But I'm trapped inside, only keep going back to the start.
What's it going to take to replace what you've left vacant?
Because you took my heart, leaving me empty.
But walls surround me.
Awake and I hear them scream.
Asleep and they provoke haunting dreams.
And I can't get out.
What's it going to take to tear them down?
Because I try to find a way.
But this place is a maze.
I try a different route every day.
But every turn leads to a dead end.
Every cry for help is a failed attempt.
Because you dropped me so low no one can hear me.
You're gone but it's like your spirit is still here haunting.
Your cruel words echo still taunting.
You created this mess, then shut the door and locked it.
Leaving me to drown in my own distress.

But I'll find my way out.
I promise I'll manage to break these walls down.
I won't let you keep me in.
Even if that's the way you like it.
I'm not here for your sick satisfaction.
I'm breaking free.
Go on and try to stop me.
But soon I'll be so high you won't be able to reach me.

You exchanged your heart for a stone.
Took your knife, cut me and didn't stop at the bone.
It used to be selflessness you showed.
But now your egoism takes the throne.

A good deed is superior to greed.

Look at you, claiming superiority.
Telling me I'm a nobody.
But when you needed me you showed no concern towards my capability.
I gave my everything, and now you proclaim you have more authority.

And you strike me where you know I am most fragile.
You use my mental health as a weapon, and say I can't win this battle.

But having been broken does not make me weak.
It actually makes me strong to have been so shattered yet still stand.

It is those who laugh at the vulnerable who are weak.

You used me like a disposable glove.
Didn't want to get your hands dirty.
Had me do the work for you, then you disposed of me.
But with all your slander, how can your conscience be clean?

A heart stops beating.

A heart breaks at goodbye.

A heart is revived.

A heart is transplanted to give another chance at life.

A new heart is witnessed at birth time.

A heart fills with love.

A heart fills with fright.

Some hearts are used like a disposable glove.

I see you like to prey on the weak.
And it just so happens you see that as me.
So you invoke on your plan of deceit.
But it's not what you think.
My courage is not what you believe.
You can't keep my soul that easily.

I can be silent and still, but cross me, and self defense becomes my will.
So go on and go for the kill.
But I will fight to not let you have that thrill.

And you've already used my mind to weaponize against me with your lies.
But my scars and my broken I'm not ashamed to deny.
So go on and use them as a weapon.
But those are the same scars that helped me strengthen.
The same scars that make my armour resilient.

Go ahead and stab me with your blade.
But my shattered pieces are also sharp; they'll leave your dagger scraped.
And your strikes are just low blows.
It's obvious you're just running in circles.
Don't know where else to go.
So you choose untruthful.

And I would've never thought it fit you so well.
You spew your lies like you're casting a spell.
But I am not a weakling as you perceive me.
Go on and keep pushing.
I won't let you claim my death a victory.

And it really hurt to know of your betrayal.
Your deception was staggeringly brutal.
I once perceived you as humble.
But now that perception has fallen low.
My disappointment in you overflows.
You're running short on morals.
I will say, meeting the real you was really painful.

But go ahead and continue to use your claws to grasp me in a tight hold.
I'll be the one to let go.

You speak of God like a holy righteous man but speak so vile of an angel.
And you do so in the presence of the ones who saw her go painfully.
Does the fact that she grew in the same womb as you have no meaning?

It is her grave you're spitting on.
Do you think it will get you to the top?
You so willingly accuse someone so wrongfully.

But what will you see when you reach the top?
Will you see heaven or fall right into hell?

What will you do when all your victims come knocking?
Locking your door won't keep their souls from haunting.

I don't believe you're actually at peace with all your
wickedness and deceit.

And after all the lies you say you still believe you walk the righteous way.

I would reach my bare hands into the blaze for those that I love.
You would first look for a fire proof glove.

All of the witch hunters came to hunt.
They came to take it all but left with none.
But I was still drowning from the damage they had already done.

And I could have let it be, and let them burn me to the ground.
But it wouldn't work to their advantage this time around.
I refused to fall into defeat.

They could bleed me vacant.
But my fight would not be taken.

I'll take my broken heart and put it back together.
Even though you're just going to take it back apart, no matter the effort.
You'll do whatever.

Give up your integrity just to see me bleed.
But you'll do so strategically, so you won't automatically kill me.
You want to do that slowly.
Fuel up on your cold needs.
And you'll do it daily like a good hygiene.

Go ahead and knock me down again, again and again.

Getting knocked down won't make me back away.
It will just make me brave.

You can keep throwing those rocks at me.
I'll just build a galaxy.

Injured hearts can heal, but *rotten ones never come back.*

I still struggle from time to time.
But that's alright.
Being imperfect is not a crime.
And at least I try.
I'm not afraid to deny.

It's you who should be ashamed for deeming me less capable just because I'm vulnerable.
That doesn't make me unstoppable.

Go ahead watch my broken wings fly.

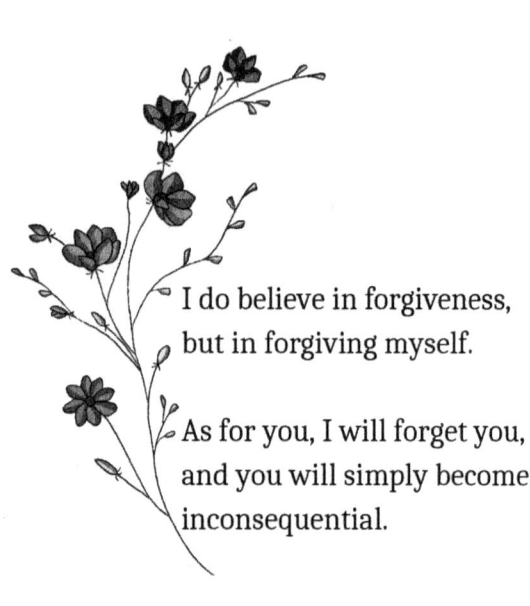

I do believe in forgiveness,
but in forgiving myself.

As for you, I will forget you,
and you will simply become
inconsequential.

I will not hate you as that will occupy space in my heart.

And you are not welcome there.

I will not allow my strength to die.
It is thoughts of you that I will allow to die.

As I removed the thorns I learned that pain can bring healing.

It's where my pain hides, where my strength also resides.
It's all those sleepless nights that awakened my might.
It's all my fright that gave me the courage to fight.
It's all those tears I cried that taught me how to swim to survive.
It's all those times I tried that had my strength amplified.
And it's all of my adversities in hindsight that showed me that even in the darkness there is light.

I watched as leaves fell from trees.
Felt like autumn was gone in a breeze.
I thought winter would freeze me in melancholy.
But then came Spring.
And everything was sprouting.
Birds were chirping.

Didn't know what they were saying, but they made beautiful melodies.
Their sounds brought my sadness to ease.

It was a fairytale, a place that no one else knows.
Magical and all to myself.
That's where I'll go when I need to be alone.

My childhood has got to be my best.
It brought me pain, but it also gave me happiness.
Summertime, playing hide-and-seek, running around and whispering into walkie talkies.
Do you still think about me?

Because I think about you sometimes.
It may not be every night.
But you still lurk in my mind.
Maybe just in distant memories.
But you're still there to remind me.

You're a faded stain on my shirt.
And yes, I've seen much worse.
But you poured drops of water into my well of hurt.
But don't worry they're not there anymore.

I grew up and they quickly evaporated.
You leaving at that time was the best thing that happened to me.

I wish you the best, though we'll never be friends.
You did damage, but it was so long ago.
When I'm reminded it's strange to believe that's a past I had known.
But believe me when I say that with no hostility.
I probably spent many years with not even the slightest thought of you.
But you're still there somehow, aren't you.

My heart was spilling
And the details were thrilling.
But to stay I thought you'd be willing.
Instead you were quick to take off running.
An unfamiliar part of you is now showing.
There's still an unhealed wound in my heart from not knowing.
Tell me now, was your heart already overflowing?

I didn't fit, but you made me believe I did, so I would just flow away.

Great seeing you again, even though it was just a run in.
But I still see you as one of my best friends.
You ask how I've been.
I want to try something new.
I don't want to pretend.
So I tell you the truth.

Messages flood your phone consecutively.
You probably don't even have time to breathe.
Sorry, I meant to say one thing, and I ended up venting.

We used to do that, remember?
We were there for each other.
I told you all my secrets.
Now I feel so undressed.
Ashamed and I only want to hide away.
I was so foolish for believing you would get me.
I told you about the dark cloud over me.
Now I see.
I get it.
It was raining, and you didn't want to get wet.

Thought you would be there til the end.
Guess not.
I held on for the sake of how it was back then.
But it's time.

Goodbye,
my fair weather friend.

You asked for a crayon, and I gave you all the colors.

Sorry—I don't come in one color.

Friends are sometimes just a trend.

Reflection

For so long I denied it.
Said it was just my insecurities.
That's what had a hold on me.
That once I learned how to love myself I'd be okay.
But I realized it wasn't that easy.
Truth is, there was so much more I was battling within.
Sudden ringing in my ears, and I couldn't breathe.
I felt cold, but I'm somehow sweating.
No reason.
My insecurities were not the only demons.

Old dreams sneak up on me from behind.
I never got to live that life.
Instead I was a statue.
Too afraid to move.
Spent years in solitude.

In a small space.
That's where I was.
That's where I stayed.
Because who could I trust?
Speaking only causes things to complicate.
So I decided to hide away.

And I say I'm not a coward, but I would have died there all because I was too afraid.

I stayed down the last time I fell.
But that's the last time I ever will.
Because I'm going to show the strength in me and not fall into defeat.

I will dream again.
Escape the nightmares I thought would never end.

And I will never be the same.
My heart will always have an ache.
But there are still many great memories to build that will continue to ease the pain.

I know I've shut a lot of doors, but I've also fought a lot of wars.

If you have at least tried, you are already a warrior in life.

Broken and torn I will not remain.
I will not only live for one day.
Soon this pain will wash away.
Inside the darkness I will not stay.

If it breaks me it also makes me.

I had everything I ever needed, but I took it for granted.

To anxiety-
You will not dictate how I live my life.

To those who have hurt me-
You will not dictate how I live my life.

I will no longer be in servitude to insecurities, fear, pain, and anxiety.

If I fall, at least I'll fall from flying.

I was agonized by the thoughts of my own mind.

It was like they threw gasoline on me, but I was the one that lit the match.

I don't want to not make it out.
I don't want to not get up when I fall.
I don't want to be the girl who has no confidence in herself.
I don't want to cry my eyes out at night.
Praying that this pain be justified.
Waiting for some victory light.

And I don't want to breathe only to survive.
Dying on the inside, giving everything its time.
Dragging the days as they go by.

I don't want to be that.

I took my brain, put it in a box, and sent it away.
Because I need my own space.
Even if it's just for a day.
It's best I leave it to meditate.
And yes, I also medicate.
I have no shame.
It's okay to seek help to find your way.
It's not a map, but a light that helps clear my sight,
lessen my fright.

My life isn't flawless.
I still carry the demons that keep me up at night.
But I also carry my fight.
And my strength I will no longer hide.
I may light a match to guide my path, but I will not ignite.
And if the candle burns, that's alright at least I tried.

And I know I'm not perfect in my ways.
I've made mistakes.
Said things I shouldn't say.

But I'll try every day to be the best version of myself.

There's a shadow that follows her around.
But she doesn't know that it's her own.
She's the one who's holding herself back most.

She doesn't see that she's her worst enemy.

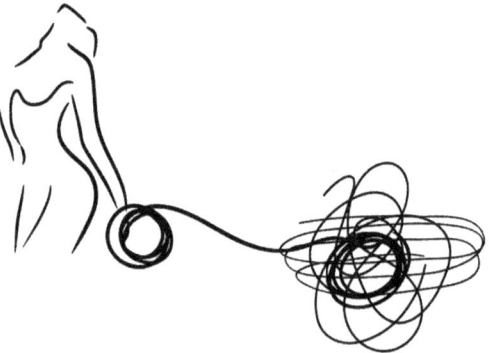

I couldn't find myself.
I got lost in everything else.
But now I'm trying to find my way back.
Trying to get my mind to relax.
Finally releasing all these demons.

My soul is still screaming.
But this dark hole I'm leaving.
I don't care what everyone else is believing, because I know my truth, and that's what I'm feeling.

I can finally say I'm escaping this place.

Goodbye, agony.
And it won't be a see you soon.
Just goodbye and rest in peace.
Because I'll be burying you, alive if I have to.

Imagine drowning for so long and then finally being able to breathe.

Though I can now breathe, my heart is still trembling from the lightning that struck me.
But I'm recovering.

At the end of the day I'm not perfectly polished.
I've got my fair amount of tarnish.

And that's okay.

There once was a little bird who had many dreams unheard, because they were only said in her head.
She had so much desire and motivation that she felt confident those dreams would be met.
Then the little bird grew up, but she never left the nest.
Mother didn't pressure her, but that was only to her own benefit.

She always had her on the tightest leash, fueling the little bird to want to break free.
Couldn't wait till eighteen.
But she swore it wasn't anxiety.
Then eighteen left.
Nineteen was a promise.
At twenty began the, "what ifs."
At twenty-one she tried to build encouragement.
But twenty two was the worst of it.
Twenty-three years, "I must deserve this."
Twenty-four, she had no idea how bad it was going to get.
Every day after she's left with regret.

Time really is one of the most valuable assets.
Are you going to sit and watch as it passes?

God gave you wings—you were meant to fly.

It was during the drought that my tear drops watered the seeds that bloomed so beautifully.

Nothing is ever wasted.

<u>Letters to heaven</u>

I used to say I wish I could have back time.
So that I could get another chance at life.
But now I wish I could have back time, so I could make everything with you right.
My sleepless nights were your sleepless nights.
You were there even when I had just made you cry.

As angry as I was that day, I also felt sorry, but instead I chose my pride.
Now I'm also sorry I didn't tell you this on that day.
I just want you to know now that even though I didn't apologize and should have, I truly was sorry.

No matter what they say, time doesn't erase.
I remember your panting breath as you ran back up the 15 steps after you went to get me medicine.
I felt awful remembering the previous day.
And I knew you had a back ache.
Little did we know then that the cancer was already growing in you.
Yet there you were running up and down the stairs for me.
No matter what, you always loved me unconditionally.

Like a lost boat at sea, you tried your best to set me sailing.
But I was never willing.
I kept on drowning.
But no matter what you never let this boat sink.
No matter how big the waves.
Even through the hurricane.
You always stayed.

And many times I was the hurricane.
I was the howling winds that would drive you insane.
I was the one that made it rain.
But you didn't care what the weatherman would say.
Nothing made a difference, you'd stay all day.

You are the only godly woman I've ever known.
I know this is the love I should have shown.
If I could have one wish, I'd choose you.
I never expressed my gratitude.
I just want you to know that I was extremely grateful.
Unfortunately, I was also ungrateful.
You deserved to be told,
>*thank you,*
>>every single day.

>*Thank you.*

I can never say those words and hold you at the same time.

I can still smell the cinnamon from Saturday mornings, as I awake to your singing.
Your rice pudding was always my favorite thing.
You could have been anywhere else, yet you were here with me.
And Sundays were for thrifting.
A trip to the flea market, just us three.

Then came breakfast at our favorite place.
We were building memories.
You were always the mother you didn't have to be.
I could shut you out, lock the door, but you always kept a spare key.
It's you who I feel when I'm feeling lonely.
It's your voice that I hear when I feel hope is far from reach.
And in everyday things it's you that I see.

I didn't know the life jacket would keep me afloat.
And that was you.
You would never let me sink.
You simply wanted me to go live my dreams.
My happy was your happy.

And you gave your everything.
I was the one lacking.

You did more than most mothers would do.
There is no other you.

I still have those sleepless nights.
But I now know what lonely really is without you by my side.
If only I could have back time.
Then maybe I wouldn't have to say, *if only.*
Now that I can't feel your warm skin, I tell you, *I love you,* every day.
Now I want to hold you close and not push you away.
Happy Birthday
Happy Mother's Day
Before, I didn't always even say.

But please know I did love you.
I do love you.
You're who I love most.
I should have given you this seed before, and like magic it would have grown.
Now I've given it to you, but it doesn't thrive on its own.
I give it all my love.
But it's not enough.
You're not here to give it your warm touch.
So what am I supposed to do without you?
I guess that's something you never taught.

You think you can imagine, but you can never know until it happens to you.

I'm the lost boat at sea, crashing into the biggest waves.
I made it through yesterday.
But will I make it through today?

Fighting the biggest storms on my own.
I used to always look for hope.
Now I realize you were the anchor I would hold.
If it weren't for you this little boat wouldn't be afloat.
I'd be at the bottom of the sea.

You are my anchor.
You are the anchor in me.

We saw you get colder every day, yet we still wished for you to stay.
But our prayers had to change.
We knew heaven was the only way.
And coincidentally it's also the greatest place.
Nothing but sunny days.
No thunderstorms with heavy rain.
No troubles to evade.
No such thing as pain.
With loved ones to meet you at the gates.
It hurt to see you in your last days, but we know there's no pain heaven can't erase.
All your faith and grace has earned you a permanent place.
And my memories of you are in many kind words full of praise.
I look up at the sky and know you are safe.
You're the dove that will meet our gaze.
A sign that you're okay.

To give hope to those who are hurting.
Letting go is not forgetting.

You are gone, but memories of you will never die.
Even when illness and age affects the mind you're forever embedded in mine.
And I wish we had more time, but know you had a long life.
I know you'll still be here as the dove that soars our skies.

I saw you fade away like a tiny boat that didn't conquer the storm at sea.
The skies were screaming.
The waves were angry vicious monsters pushing you around relentlessly.
You kept gasping for air, but you were drowning.
The waters were rising.
My precious Grandmother, you got tired of swimming.

But that does not make you weak.
Your strength is one of the greatest things I've ever seen.

I know your strength to let go was the most difficult.

I watched the garden grow beautifully.
Little did I know it would soon be overcome by weeds.
It was your presence that made it a beautiful scene.
And it's your absence that now makes the flowers suddenly not matter to me.

I no longer care if the grass is green.
The shriveled petals gather and declare the wind a vicious thing.
The birds no longer desire to sing.
I hear arguing between the grass and trees.
They're going off about who is more deserving.
Each one wants the last drink.

And the honeybees cry for the seeds that they will never see sprouting.
The butterflies proclaim their beauty is too great and leave.
The withering roses wish for the sun to stop shining.
They beg the clouds to start dancing.
Hope they fight just so the skies start crying.
The trees wait anxiously and strangle the hibiscus just so they can get every sip.

Even in adversity their desire to thrive still exists.
And it gives me a reason why as a witness.

The flowers will bloom

I'll pick up your broken pieces, I'm not afraid to get cut.
I have sharp pieces of my own, and some are the words people have thrown.

I know pain very well, we're more than just acquainted.
We're intertwined like we're fated.
I'm strong enough to survive, I've got the scars to prove it.
Let me show you that the broken can be mended.
Your fear can be boxed up and surrendered.

We'll bury it if you'd like.
And welcome your newborn strength to life.
You may not always win the fight, but your strength and hope never have to die.

Waterfalls in my dreams, my tears cascading.
But not in a way to provoke a haunting scheme yet a beautiful thing.
All of the animals of the forest gather to see.
The sun shines bright over me, making sure to light the scene.
And it's my tears that nature's creatures drink.

What almost killed me is now nourishing.
My tears are helping strength revive.
They cascade splashing at the soil causing blooms left and right.
In the forest I lie, and it is my broken that is giving life.

City lights lighting up the night sky.
People racing trying to fight time.
It just never seems to be enough, and that's just life.
We try to get things right, put up a fight.
But it seems like a useless try.
So we let out a sigh and retry.
Because the stars are still going to shine.
And the sun will rise.
And there will be days when your emotions collide.
But there will always be that light, even when it's out of sight.
You just have to choose to want to be alright.

The waves grew stronger and stronger trying to climb over the boat.
Forcefully rocking it back and forth.

The sky cried in violent storms.
The winds screamed in desperate howls.
The boat knew that even boats can drown.

Help,
the boat pleaded in defeat.
The anchor said,
don't worry, take sanctuary in me.

As the anchor dropped the boat felt hope that the storm would win not.
The anchor screamed,
have faith in me, I will prevail.
And when it did, in triumph the boat set off to sail.

Isn't it strange when you see someone you know after not seeing them for sometime, but instead of saying hi you just walk on right past by?
Even after looking one another in the eyes.
Why are we pretending?
Kind of condescending.
Don't you think, on both of our parts?
Because I wonder if you see me differently now, and I'm not good enough for you.

But maybe you think the same about me.

Why are we servitude to our insecurities?

We are much more powerful than the negative comments.
Yet the ones we don't believe are compliments.
And instead we dissect harsh words we speak to ourselves
and consume all of their contents.

But we are much more powerful than the chains of our
own negative thoughts.
We can break free.

When did we become so obsessed with society's perception of how we look?

We used to ride bikes.
Now we measure our thighs.
We used to play with dirt.
Now we complain about ruining our skirts.
We used to love the rain.
Now we complain about a humid day.
We used to come home with rocks in our hair.
Now we worry about what to wear.
We used to climb trees.
Now we count our flaws relentlessly.

When will we learn to wholeheartedly love the reflection we see?

Know that you are beautiful.
Know you are worth much more.

But not only because of someone who told you.

No one can say it better to you than yourself.

Mending the pieces of our broken selves.
When will we learn to move on without it being with someone else?
Or only a matter of time will tell?

Let's float instead of falling.
Let's choose instead of willing.

Even though you are hurting, know you are worthy.

Your scars do not define who you are but how you became.

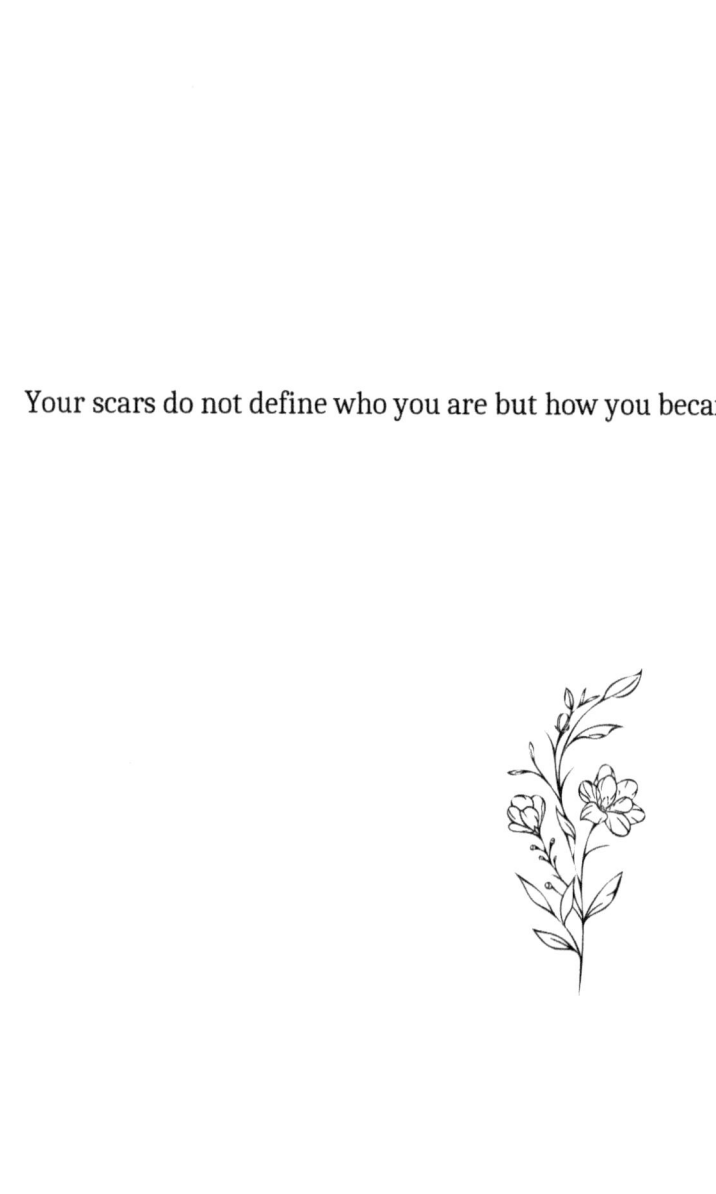

Staying strong is one of the best pieces of advice you can take.
Even though it's a cliche.

Because no matter what you go through, it will be over eventually.
And it's up to you whether you will be standing at the end or on the ground when it's over.

I know it's hard when everything falls apart.

But know in your heart that it will be okay.
The pain won't forever stay.

Stay strong even when life makes you fragile.
Stay up even when life makes it easy for you to fall down.

There is struggle, there is pain, but through it all strength is gained.

The lights flicker and startle you suddenly.
And that's quite sincerely a part of you I hadn't seen.

It's a softness to your coarse edge.
A surprise to those who say you're heartless.
Because I heard it.
That pounding coming from your chest.
It's not a weakness.
Lying is actually the easiest, but showing your vulnerability is the hardest.
So go on and show me your distress.
I'm here for it.
No judgement on my end.

Only open arms so show me your heart.
Your flaws are a work of art.
And I'm ready to catch you if you fall apart.
We'll mend your pieces back together to show just how strong you are.

It's good to reach out to someone for help.
But if you don't, that doesn't mean you have to battle alone.
You're never alone in a battle.
You always have yourself.

When you're battling something reach within yourself, and grab hold of your anchor, which is your strength.
Grab hold of that to keep you firm.
To keep you steadfast.

Receiving love from someone else can be a crutch to your broken heart.
But by receiving love from yourself you will learn to walk again, and heal your broken heart.

In the darkest days, when you're feeling so lonely, so afraid, you have to find hope and be brave.
And even though your heart aches, you can't let it be the last say.

You have to be strong, as cliche as it seems, continue to hold on.
Know that the ache will go away.

Don't let yourself drown in your tears.
Hope is always near.
And in the midst of it all, you will find that you will fall, but you can get back up.

And where you don't see a light, you put a light.
And that light may be dimmer than ever, but soon it will be shining bright.

Don't hold it all inside.
You'll die a little more each time.

You have to let it out.
Reach out.

Release the pain.
Don't restrain.

Because you'll hold it all in, and one day you'll break.

Words don't fix everything, but they can give your heart hope.

So choose your words carefully.
The ones you speak to yourself especially.

To those who judge you, let it be their game.
It's your life, you will always have the final say.

The decision was one that would hurt, but it was also one that would heal.

You realize that once it's dawn, yesterday is forever gone.
What's done is done.
You can't go back.
So why keep reliving it?
If it can be fixed, that's great.

But when you realize you can't have back yesterday, don't let yourself drain.

When your heart wants to let go, don't let it do so.
Even when it's difficult.
Remember hope.

She tries hard to keep her place.
She doesn't run or hide away.

I am like the drought, longing for rain.
But I am also like the rain begging for the sun.
I am the flood looking for a way to drain.
I am the howling wind, wondering when the calm will come.

I am winter dreading the cold.
And I am summer dying of thirst.
But I am also the bird flying despite its wings being hurt.

I am the roots that dig deep when the sky doesn't provide.
I am the fear in search of light.
I am my own knight.
I am the howls of the night.
I am the sun that knows I have to rise despite the struggles of life.

And I have also been the monster that haunts my own mind.
The words that strike me where it most hurts.
I am my own ghost that lurks.
I am the healing and the injuries.

I am my own armor, but also the dagger.
I am the sorrow concealed by laughter.
When it is today, I am tomorrow.
I am a sunny day but also a natural disaster.
The hurricane and the landfall that causes it to dissipate.
I am my own anchor but also the sweeping waves.

I am the blooms but also the decay.
I am insanity, and I'm also sane.
I am the hope when I no longer want to try.
I am the relief and the disappointed sigh.
I am a human, like everyone else, running on time.
But I will always be the fight no matter how hard I'm hit by life.

Strong doesn't mean you can't get knocked down.
Strong is getting up after you've been knocked down.

Time you'll never get back.
So cherish it, and make memories that will forever last.

Threads of me everywhere.
I wish I could stitch myself to your heart and forever stay there.

Needle pricks to my skin softened by your kiss.
You declare to me your love and all your promises.
We're dancing in bliss.

And the butterflies synchronize.
It's a moment of frozen time.
It's the rest of the world, and then there's you and I.
We experience sunshine and moonlight.
Our love is so great that even when our souls die it will continue to live in another life.

I only knew of the light from fairy tales.
I lived in the dark until I met you.
You're my angel who pulled me right out of hell.
The one who made what I believed impossible true.
You taught me to not be afraid, assured me you'd be there if I fell.

You lit the sky for me.
Gave me strength when I was weak.
And when I couldn't walk you carried me.
Lent me your eyes when I couldn't see.
Gave me air when I couldn't breathe.
You are my anchor when I'm the lost boat battling the storms at sea.

You've already seen me through the worst, yet you're still ready to face more.
You say together there's nothing we can't conquer.
You treat my heart with such delicacy.
Look at me as if I were an exquisite thing.
Your hands feel like brush strokes to my skin painting me as if I were an art piece.

You trace my scars as if they were art.
You include my tears in every brush stroke.
You keep me steady when the violent winds blow.
And you paint me in violet, and call me yours.
You're not afraid to get pricked as you remove my thorns.

And the touch of your lips feel as if you worship my every little bit.
In every kiss I feel your promises.
My once flowerless heart is full of blooms all because of you.

You're not like the flowers but like the butterflies and hummingbirds that help them thrive.
Like the sunlight who brings their beauty to life.
Like the water capable of reviving a petal so shriveled ready to give up the fight.
Like the fertilizer providing all the nutrients to help them reach their maximum height.

You are the gentle hands that press upon the soil keeping it together.
You are the gentle hands that collect my shriveled petals but not to have them disposed.
You use them as compost.
You tell me you will turn my broken into something beautiful.
You spread my fragments across the garden, and we watch as beautiful blooms grow.
Others have simply deemed my flaws unusable.
But you have shown me that even in the shattered there is still hope.

You are those vigilant eyes, always seeking to see if I'm alright.
You are much more than a flower in my eyes.
You are the gardener who gives the entire garden life.

You are my gardener who gives me love, warmth and helps me grow.
My lover, my home.

Ask me for crystals, and I will give you diamonds.
Ask me for a star, and I will give you a constellation.

Ask me for water in a jar, and I will give you an ocean.
To the one that's deserving, I will give my entire heart and devotion.

Like the darkness of the night the hurt resurfaces after daylight.
And every single scar that lies beneath your wounded heart has now become a part of who you are.
A scratch on the surface became a hole that went all the way through.
It took away all the great things that you knew.
While the pain grew and grew.
The wind blew so hard.
And you were already fragile, so it knocked you down.
But this time you don't want to get up.
Just want to give up.
Your dreams have now turned to dust.
But holding on is a must.

There will be greater things that will be brand new.
Your strength also grew.

And let the wind blow.
You've become a master at grabbing hold.

And you were also made from dust.
So pick your dreams back up.

I will protect and nourish you.
I will feed you love and kind words.
Your feelings will never go unheard.

I will shield you from harm.
And when you are alarmed, I will hold you to calm.

I will embrace you with so much love.
You will be wrapped in devotion that everywhere you walk you will feel embraced by my hug.

After all you are my warrior, who never gave up on me.
My dearest heart, I will treat you with kindness for as long as you continue to beat.

Dear reader,

Thank you for reading my book. I hope you enjoyed it!

If you have a moment, I'd really appreciate it if you could leave your honest review and/or rating on Amazon.
Reviews help other readers decide whether my book is right for them, while also supporting me as an indie author.

You can scan the QR code below to be directed to the Amazon review page.

I'd love to hear your thoughts.

    With gratitude,

       Cynthia

www.ingramcontent.com/pod-product-compliance
Lightning Source LLC
Chambersburg PA
CBHW070847050426
42453CB00012B/2079